Why you should smile

Happiness is one of the most beautiful thing in life

Happiness is one of the most beautiful thing in life

By

Ijezie Beyonce

Introduction

- The Universal Language of Smiles
- The Purpose of This Book

Table of content
Introduction

Chapter one:

People who are happy are more productive.

Once upon a time in the bustling city of Progressville, where the corporate world never slept and the pursuit of success was a way of life, there was a man named William. William was not your typical executive; he was a firm believer in the idea that people who are happy are more productive.

William was the CEO of a thriving technology company, and he had earned a reputation for being a brilliant leader who understood the extraordinary power of happiness. He had always believed that the traditional corporate environment, with its emphasis on deadlines and targets, often overlooked the simple yet profound connection between happiness and productivity.

William's journey to understanding the significance of happiness in the workplace began with a personal revelation. Early in his career, he had experienced a period of burnout and stress. The long hours and relentless pursuit of success had taken a toll on his health and well-being.

It was during a weekend getaway in a serene countryside cabin that William had his epiphany. As he gazed at the peaceful surroundings, he realized that his relentless pursuit of success had left him feeling empty and unfulfilled. In contrast, the tranquil setting, filled with the simple joys of nature, had given him a sense of happiness and contentment.

This revelation sparked a change in William. He returned to the corporate world with a new vision. He believed that creating a work environment that prioritized employee happiness was not just a moral obligation but a strategic move for success. And so, he began to implement changes in his company that focused on fostering happiness among his employees.

William's approach had a profound impact on productivity:

1. **Motivation:** Happy employees were more motivated. They felt a sense of purpose and were eager to contribute to the company's success.

2. **Innovation:** A happy workplace fostered innovation. Employees were more likely to think creatively and come up with new ideas.

3. **Collaboration:** Happiness led to improved collaboration. When people felt good about their work environment, they were more inclined to work together and share ideas.

4. **Stress Reduction:** A focus on happiness reduced workplace stress. Employees were better equipped to handle challenges and setbacks.

5. **Employee Retention:** Happy employees were more likely to stay with the company. This reduced turnover and saved the company recruitment and training costs.

Over time, Progressville became known for its progressive approach to the corporate world. William's company thrived, and other businesses in the city followed suit, recognizing that fostering happiness among employees was a winning strategy.

The story of William and Progressville serves as a testament to the idea that people who are happy are more productive. It reminds us that the pursuit of success should not come at the cost of well-being but rather be a journey that integrates happiness and productivity. In a world where work often takes precedence, William's story shows that a happy workforce is not just a dream but a reality that benefits both individuals and the companies they serve.

Who, in your opinion, accomplishes more in a typical day?
 Who is more optimistic, content, and driven, the person who complains and rants about how unfair his life is or the person who is driven?
 In general, happy people are more productive and more likely to achieve their objectives than unhappy people.

When you're happy and content, you tend to have a more positive outlook on life. This positivity can extend to your work and tasks, making you more enthusiastic and motivated to get things done.

Happiness often brings increased energy and vitality. With more energy, you can tackle tasks with greater focus and efficiency, leading to improved productivity.

Happy individuals tend to be more resilient in the face of challenges and setbacks. They are better equipped to bounce back from difficulties, which can lead to a more consistent and productive work performance.

Happiness can enhance creativity and problem-solving skills. When you're in a good mood, your brain is more likely to think outside the box, leading to innovative solutions and increased productivity.

Happy people generally take better care of their physical and mental health. This improved health can lead to increased productivity by reducing absenteeism and enhancing cognitive functioning.

Happy people tend to have better interpersonal relationships. Positive relationships with colleagues and peers can lead to more collaborative and efficient work environments, ultimately boosting productivity.

Happiness can reduce stress levels. When you're less stressed, you can focus more on your tasks, make better decisions, and work more productively.

Happy individuals often set and achieve goals more effectively. They are motivated by a sense of fulfillment and satisfaction, which can lead to increased productivity in both personal and professional endeavors.

Happy people are more likely to manage their time efficiently. They can prioritize tasks, set clear goals, and complete projects in a timely manner, contributing to greater productivity.

A positive and happy mindset can help you approach problems with a clear and creative mindset. You are more likely to find effective solutions to challenges, leading to increased productivity.

Happiness is associated with better decision-making skills. When you're in a good mood, you are more likely to make rational and effective choices, which can positively impact your productivity.

Happiness often acts as a natural motivator. Happy individuals are driven by their sense of contentment and well-being, which can lead to higher levels of motivation and, subsequently, increased productivity.

There is a strong link between happiness and productivity. When you're happy, you're more likely to approach tasks with enthusiasm, energy, and a positive mindset.

This can lead to improved efficiency and effectiveness in various aspects of your life, including work and personal projects. Smiling is one of the outward expressions of happiness, and it can contribute to these positive effects.

Chapter two:
People in your life care about you and rely on you.

In the picturesque village of Carehaven, nestled amidst rolling hills and charming cottages, the residents understood the profound connection between smiles and the people in their lives who cared about them and relied on them. Carehaven was a place where strong bonds and support systems thrived, and smiles played a central role in this community's way of life.

The story of Carehaven began with a woman named Emma, a devoted mother who exemplified the idea that people in your life care about you and rely on you. Emma had always been known for her radiant smile and her unwavering commitment to her family and friends.

Emma's journey to understanding the significance of smiles began with her own family. She was the matriarch of a large and loving family that included her children, grandchildren, and many friends. Her home was a warm and inviting place where laughter and smiles were abundant.

One day, as her eldest grandchild, Sophie, faced a particularly challenging period in her life, Emma made it her mission to offer unwavering support and encouragement. Sophie was dealing with school pressures, friendship troubles, and the general difficulties of growing up. She felt overwhelmed and lost.

But whenever Sophie visited Emma, she was met with a warm and understanding smile. Emma listened attentively to Sophie's concerns and offered guidance with kindness and a gentle smile. Emma's smile was more than a simple gesture; it was a beacon of support and love.

As the years passed, Emma came to understand the incredible role that smiles played in her relationships:

1. **Emotional Support:** Emma's smiles were a source of emotional support. Her family and friends knew they could rely on her for empathy and understanding, which strengthened their connections.

2. **Building Trust:** Emma's warm smiles fostered trust. People felt comfortable opening up to her, knowing that they would be met with compassion and love.

3. **Conflict Resolution:** In moments of disagreement, Emma's smile diffused tension. She approached disputes with a smile, encouraging understanding and compromise.

4. **Acts of Kindness:** Emma's smiles inspired acts of kindness. Her family and friends often went out of their way to support each other, creating a cycle of shared happiness and support.

5. **Strengthening Bonds:** Emma's commitment to her loved ones, coupled with her warm smiles, deepened the bonds within her community.

Emma's impact on Carehaven was profound. Her family, friends, and neighbors all embraced the idea that smiles were not just expressions of personal happiness but also powerful tools for building and maintaining strong relationships.

Carehaven was a place where people smiled not just for themselves but also for the loved ones who cared about them and relied on them. The story of Emma and the residents of Carehaven was a reminder to the world that the power of a smile extended beyond personal joy; it had the potential to create a network of love and support that made life richer and more meaningful.

Who are your most significant relationships? Chances would say you'd are, do anything for these people, isn't that so?
This is a good place to start if you want something to make you happy.
There will always be someone who loves you unconditionally, no matter how bad life gets.
Do you believe that your loved ones would like to see you miserable and unhappy? Naturally, they do not.
Therefore, select happiness for your loved ones. It will greatly enhance the enjoyment of your relationships.

When you smile, you convey a positive and approachable demeanor. People are naturally drawn to those who radiate positivity, and they are more likely to care about and want to be around you.

Smiling is a universal sign of trustworthiness. When you smile, you signal to others that you are friendly and open, which can lead to increased trust in your relationships. Trust is a fundamental element in any healthy, caring relationship.

Smiles can help reduce stress, both for you and those around you. When people perceive you as a source of positivity and stress relief, they are more likely to turn to you for support and rely on your presence in their lives.

Smiles facilitate smoother and more effective communication. When you smile during conversations, it shows that you're engaged, approachable, and interested in what the other person is saying. This can lead to more meaningful and caring interactions.

Your smile can serve as a positive influence on others. When people see you smiling and maintaining a positive outlook, they may be inspired to do the same. This, in turn, can create a network of mutual support and positivity.

In times of conflict or difficulty, a smile can act as a bridge to resolution. Your willingness to approach conflicts with a positive attitude can lead to more constructive and caring solutions to problems.

Smiling can improve your own mood, making you a more pleasant and enjoyable person to be around. People naturally gravitate towards those who make them feel good and cared for.

When you smile at others and demonstrate care and empathy, it often encourages them to reciprocate with the same feelings of care and reliance. By being caring and approachable, you can foster a supportive network of relationships.

Smiling can create a stronger emotional connection between you and the people in your life. It signals that you are empathetic, understanding, and emotionally available, which are qualities that make others feel cared for and supported.

A smile makes you more approachable. People are more likely to seek your advice, support, and companionship if they perceive you as someone who is easy to approach and talk to.

Smiling is a powerful tool for building and maintaining caring, reliable relationships. It fosters positivity, trust, and open communication, making you a person that others naturally gravitate towards for support and companionship.

Chapter three:
More happy people are needed in the world.

In a world filled with hustle and bustle, stress, and countless distractions, there was a growing need for more happiness. And the residents of a small town known as Merrysville understood that one of the simplest and most effective ways to infuse happiness into the world was through smiles.

Merrysville was not a place of extravagant riches or extraordinary events. It was a place where everyday people recognized the extraordinary power of a simple smile. The town was known for its cheerful atmosphere, and its residents believed that they could make a significant difference in the world by spreading happiness one smile at a time.

One of Merrysville's most beloved inhabitants was a young woman named Lily. Lily was not particularly affluent, nor was she famous, but she possessed a remarkable gift – her infectious smile. Everywhere she went, her warm and genuine smile brightened people's days.

Lily had a story of her own. She had once experienced a period of profound sadness and despair. During those dark days, she had felt isolated and lost. It was her best friend, Sarah, who had introduced her to the power of a simple smile. Sarah had reminded Lily that even in the most challenging moments, a smile could create a glimmer of light.

The lesson stuck with Lily, and she made it her mission to bring happiness to the world. With a smile on her face and a twinkle in her eye, she greeted people she met on the street, in shops, and at community gatherings. Her smile was her gift to others, and it had a ripple effect:

1. **Acts of Kindness:** Lily's smiles often inspired acts of kindness. When people encountered her warm and cheerful demeanor, they were more likely to perform random acts of kindness for others.

2. **Improved Social Connections:** Her smiles encouraged open and friendly social interactions. People in Merrysville were approachable and felt more connected to one another, deepening the sense of community.

3. **Stress Reduction:** Lily's presence helped reduce stress and anxiety. Her smiles acted as a natural stress reliever, making people feel at ease and uplifted.

4. **Positive Outlook:** Her consistent optimism and smiles inspired others to see the world with a more positive perspective. Residents of Merrysville began to appreciate life's small joys.

As time passed, Merrysville's reputation for its cheerful and kind-hearted residents spread beyond its borders. The town had become a beacon of hope and happiness in the world. People from neighboring towns visited to experience the magic of Merrysville, and some even decided to make it their home.

The story of Lily in Merrysville was a reminder to the world that more happy people were needed. It taught everyone that happiness was not something reserved for the privileged or the famous; it was something that could be shared with a simple smile. In a world that often seemed chaotic and overwhelming, Merrysville's residents showed that happiness could be a collective effort, one smile at a time.

We seem to hear about a new tragedy every week that makes us question the human spirit. Sadly, we live in a world where war, famine, poverty, and destruction are unavoidable. But here is the problem: Ego always wins out.
One happy person's actions can spread throughout the world and literally change everything. So be the change you wish to make. Choose contentment.

Make the most of this moment. This is the time of your life.

Smiling can play a crucial role in creating a more positive and happier world by inspiring and encouraging happiness in others.

Happiness is contagious. When you smile, it's more likely that others around you will mirror your positive emotions. This spreads happiness to those who may need it most.

Smiling fosters positive social interactions and strong relationships. By smiling at others, you can make them feel valued, appreciated, and happier, strengthening connections.

Smiles are contagious. When you smile at someone, they are more likely to smile back. This creates a positive feedback loop where happiness spreads from person to person. By sharing your smile, you can uplift the moods of those around you.

Smiling can help reduce stress and anxiety. When you smile, your brain releases feel-good neurotransmitters like dopamine and endorphins, which can lower stress levels. When you're less stressed, you're better equipped to handle challenges and contribute positively to the world.

Smiles are a universal sign of friendliness and approachability. When you smile, you're more likely to make new friends and strengthen existing relationships. Positive relationships are a key component of overall happiness.

Smiling can actually improve your mood. It's a simple and accessible way to boost your own happiness. When you smile, even if it's forced at first, your brain interprets it as a sign of happiness and begins to release those aforementioned feel-good chemicals.

When conflicts arise, approaching them with a smile and a positive attitude can often defuse tension and lead to more amicable resolutions. Smiling can promote understanding and compromise

Smiling can help reduce stress and anxiety. When you smile, your brain releases feel-good neurotransmitters like dopamine and endorphins, which can lower stress levels. When you're less stressed, you're better equipped to handle challenges and contribute positively to the world.

Smiles are a universal sign of friendliness and approachability. When you smile, you're more likely to make new friends and strengthen existing relationships. Positive relationships are a key component of overall happiness.

Smiling can actually improve your mood. It's a simple and accessible way to boost your own happiness. When you smile, even if it's forced at first, your brain interprets it as a sign of happiness and begins to release those aforementioned feel-good chemicals.

Smiling has been linked to various health benefits, including lower blood pressure, a stronger immune system, and increased longevity. A happier and healthier populace contributes to a better world.

Chapter four:
You are well.

In the quiet town of Wellnessville, nestled amidst rolling hills and pristine nature, people lived by the belief that "You are well." This phrase was not just a greeting; it was a way of life, a reminder that well-being extended beyond the absence of illness. In Wellnessville, people understood that smiles played a crucial role in their overall wellness.

The story of Wellnessville revolved around a woman named Sarah, who had a profound realization about the connection between smiles and well-being. Sarah had always been a cheerful soul, but her journey began during a challenging period in her life.

She faced a series of personal and professional setbacks that left her feeling overwhelmed and unwell. It was during this difficult time that she discovered the phrase "You are well" painted on a sign near the entrance to Wellnessville. The message intrigued her, and she decided to explore the town.

As she ventured deeper into Wellnessville, she noticed something remarkable: the townspeople seemed genuinely content and contentment radiated from their warm smiles. Curious, Sarah struck up conversations with them, and they all shared their perspective on why they believed they were well.

Sarah's interactions with the residents of Wellnessville led to a profound realization. She understood that smiles were not just expressions of happiness; they were acknowledgments of wellness in the present moment. Sarah's journey had taught her that "You are well" wasn't a distant goal to strive for, but a recognition of the well-being that already existed within.

As Sarah embraced this philosophy, she discovered that smiles were not just indicators of well-being; they also played a central role in maintaining it:

1. **Positive Outlook:** Smiles fostered a positive outlook on life. The act of smiling encouraged a mindset of gratitude and contentment, which were essential components of overall well-being.

2. **Stress Reduction:** Smiles were a natural stress-reliever. They reduced stress hormones and promoted relaxation, which was crucial for wellness.

3. **Strong Social Bonds:** Smiles built strong social bonds. In Wellnessville, close-knit relationships contributed to residents' emotional well-being, and smiles played a key role in creating these connections.

4. **Healthy Lifestyle:** People in Wellnessville maintained healthy habits. Smiles inspired individuals to engage in exercise, maintain a balanced diet, and prioritize self-care, all of which contributed to their well-being.

Sarah's transformation inspired others in Wellnessville. The town had always been a haven of well-being, but Sarah's journey led to a deepening of the philosophy, where the connection between well-being and smiles was celebrated and cherished.

Wellnessville was not just a place; it was a way of life, a reminder that the phrase "You are well" was not a destination but a recognition of the wellness that existed in the present moment. It taught the world that well-being could be achieved and maintained through the simple, powerful act of smiling and acknowledging that well-being began with the recognition that "You are well."

There is one thing you can be thankful for no matter how sick, tired, sad, or unhappy you are: the fact that you are still here. On a regular basis, loved ones leave us unexpectedly. Consider what you would do if you knew today would be your last?
 Would you spend it dwelling on all the things you don't have?
Most likely not. You would try to spend time with the people you care about most to unwind, laugh, and live.
Smiling triggers the release of endorphins, even for healthy individuals. This can lead to an immediate boost in mood, making you feel even better about your well-being.

Smiling can lower stress levels by decreasing the production of stress-related hormones. Even when you're doing well, life can still present challenges, and smiling helps you manage stress more effectively.

Smiling encourages a more optimistic outlook on life, which can enhance your overall sense of well-being. This positive perspective can help you maintain your good health and mental well-being.

Healthy individuals who smile frequently can create stronger and more positive social connections. These relationships can further support your overall well-being

Smiling can boost cognitive functions like problem-solving, creativity, and decision-making. This can contribute to your well-being by helping you make better decisions and solve problems more effectively.

Smiling often involves relaxed facial muscles and a lower heart rate. This physical relaxation can contribute to your overall sense of well-being, promoting relaxation and calm.

A simple smile is an act of kindness that can brighten someone else's day, even when you're already well. It's a way to share positivity and contribute to the well-being of others.

Smiling is associated with an enhanced immune system, which is essential for maintaining good health. A strong immune system can help prevent illnesses and keep you feeling your best.

Smiling can boost self-confidence, even for those who are already well. This confidence can help you approach life's challenges with a positive and proactive mindset.

Maintaining a positive outlook and engaging in acts of kindness, such as smiling, has been linked to longer life and better overall health.

Smiling can add an extra layer of well-being and happiness to the lives of individuals who are already healthy. It can improve mood, reduce stress, enhance cognitive function, and promote strong social connections, all of which contribute to an overall sense of well-being and happiness.

Chapter five
Healthy people are happy ones.

In the peaceful village of Wellsville, nestled in the heart of fertile green valleys and pristine lakes, the villagers cherished a simple yet profound belief: that healthy people are happy ones. Their way of life revolved around the idea that physical and emotional well-being were intricately connected, and their smiles played a central role in this philosophy.

The village's story began with a wise elder named Martha, who had spent her life studying the interplay between health and happiness. She understood that smiles were not just expressions of joy but also a reflection of a person's overall well-being.

Martha's journey had a personal touch. In her youth, she had battled health issues and had experienced the challenges of maintaining happiness in the face of physical ailments. It was during this time that she began to explore the connections between smiles and health.

Martha learned that smiles had a profound impact on well-being:

1. **Endorphin Release:** Smiles triggered the release of endorphins, the body's natural mood elevators. These endorphins not only improved mood but also enhanced the body's overall sense of well-being.

2. **Stress Reduction:** Smiles were a natural stress-reliever. They reduced stress hormones, calmed the nervous system, and led to better mental and physical health.

3. **Positive Outlook:** Smiles fostered a positive outlook on life. People who smiled regularly were more optimistic, resilient, and better equipped to handle life's challenges.

4. **Social Connections:** Smiles encouraged social connections, creating a support network that was essential for emotional and physical well-being.

5. **Healthy Habits:** Martha found that people who smiled often were more likely to engage in healthy habits. They were more motivated to exercise, maintain a balanced diet, and take better care of themselves.

Martha shared her knowledge with the villagers of Wellsville, who embraced her wisdom wholeheartedly. They saw the incredible connection between smiles and health and decided to make it a central part of their lives.

Wellsville soon became known for its thriving, vibrant community of healthy and happy individuals. The village's emphasis on well-being didn't just lead to physical health but also emotional health. Residents smiled more, and their smiles were not just an expression of personal joy; they were a reflection of their overall vitality and happiness.

The story of Wellsville was a testament to the idea that healthy people are happy ones. It showed that a genuine, warm smile could be a reflection of not just personal happiness but also a person's commitment to their own well-being. It was a reminder to the world that smiles were not just symbols of joy but also powerful tools for achieving and maintaining good health and happiness.

Here is a good reason to be happy right now if you need any more: Happiness is directly linked to health, according to research. Compared to those who are unhappy, people who are happy tend to exercise more and eat healthier.

The quality of your thoughts determines your level of happiness in life: subsequently, monitor in like manner, and take care that you engage no ideas unsatisfactory to excellence and sensible natural

Smiling triggers the release of endorphins, which act as natural mood lifters. Even for already healthy individuals, this reduction in stress hormones and the release of endorphins can further enhance their sense of happiness and relaxation.

Smiling is a simple way to improve your mood, even if you're already feeling happy. It can amplify your positive emotions and create a more profound sense of well-being.

Happy individuals who smile frequently tend to have a more optimistic perspective on life. This positive outlook can boost their overall happiness and resilience in the face of challenges.

Smiling makes people appear more approachable and friendly. Healthy individuals can use their smiles to foster positive social interactions and build stronger connections with others, contributing to their overall happiness.

Smiling can create a positive feedback loop. The more you smile, the more you tend to receive positive responses from others. This reinforces your happiness and leads to a deeper sense of well-being.

Smiling can improve cognitive functions, such as problem-solving and creativity, for healthy individuals. This mental agility can enhance their overall sense of happiness.

Smiling is associated with a boost in the immune system, even for healthy individuals. A strong immune system can help prevent illnesses and keep individuals feeling their best.

Smiling often involves relaxed facial muscles and a lower heart rate. This physical relaxation can contribute to overall well-being and a sense of calm.

A simple smile is an act of kindness that can brighten someone else's day. Healthy individuals can use their smiles to create positive experiences for others and share happiness.

Studies suggest that individuals who maintain a positive outlook on life and who are generally happy tend to live longer and enjoy better overall health. Smiling can be a part of this overall happiness strategy.

For already healthy and happy individuals, smiling can be an additional tool for maintaining and enhancing their well-being. It can provide a sense of relaxation, improve mood, and contribute to a more positive and fulfilling life.

Chapter six:

Relationships between happy people are stronger.

In the lively neighborhood of Joyville, people understood the profound connection between happiness and the strength of their relationships. This was a place where smiles were not just a reflection of joy but also the glue that bound people together.

At the heart of Joyville lived a couple, Emily and Thomas, who epitomized the idea that relationships between happy people were stronger. Their story was a testament to how smiles could create unbreakable bonds and shared happiness.

Emily and Thomas had been high school sweethearts who had fallen in love on a sunny afternoon. Their love story was marked by laughter, shared dreams, and the warmth of their smiles. They believed in the power of happiness, and it was this belief that allowed them to build a beautiful life together.

Over the years, Emily and Thomas encountered their fair share of challenges. Life brought its ups and downs, but they approached each obstacle with a smile. They embraced the idea that happiness was not just a destination but a journey they could share.

Their home in Joyville was a haven of joy and laughter. They were known for their frequent gatherings, where friends and family would come together, sharing stories, laughter, and, of course, smiles. It was during these gatherings that their philosophy truly shone.

The happiness and positivity that Emily and Thomas exuded had a profound impact on their relationships:

1. **Open Communication:** Their home was a place where open communication thrived. Smiles created an atmosphere of trust and encouraged family and friends to express themselves freely.

2. **Resilience:** Emily and Thomas's shared optimism allowed them to overcome challenges with grace. They believed in each other and leaned on their shared happiness during tough times.

3. **Conflict Resolution:** Smiles diffused conflicts. Instead of escalating disputes, they approached them with a sense of empathy, humor, and a willingness to compromise.

4. **Strong Social Network:** Their gatherings created a strong social network. Friends and family were drawn to their warm and positive atmosphere, deepening the bonds within their community.

5. **Acts of Kindness:** Their happiness inspired acts of kindness. Friends and family members often went out of their way to support one another and make each other smile, creating a cycle of shared happiness.

As the years passed, Joyville became a place where the residents understood that relationships between happy people were stronger. The neighborhood thrived on the idea that shared happiness created bonds that were unbreakable.

The story of Emily and Thomas in Joyville was a reminder that happiness was not just a personal pursuit; it was a shared experience that could strengthen relationships. It taught the residents of Joyville that a warm smile was not only an expression of personal joy but also the key to nurturing stronger, more resilient, and happier relationships.

The majority of surveys show that married people are happier than single people.
 That doesn't mean you should be hitched to accomplish bliss.
It means that when you choose to be happy, you are more likely to have better relationships with friends, family, and other loved ones as well as better relationships at work.

When both individuals in a relationship are happy and frequently smile, it creates a positive feedback loop. Each person's happiness reinforces the other's, leading to an atmosphere of joy and contentment within the relationship.
Smiles promote shared positive experiences. When happy individuals exchange smiles, it fosters a sense of connection and shared happiness, making their bond stronger.

Smiling is a nonverbal form of communication that signals warmth, openness, and interest. When both partners smile during conversations, it leads to better and more effective communication, fostering understanding and connection

Happy individuals are more likely to support and uplift each other. Smiles can be a way to express this support and reassure each other during both joyful moments and challenging times.

Happy individuals tend to approach conflicts with a more positive and constructive attitude. When they smile and maintain a positive outlook, it's easier to resolve disagreements in a respectful and harmonious manner.

Happy individuals often share common values and outlooks on life, which can strengthen the foundation of their relationship. This shared happiness can lead to a more fulfilling and enduring connection.

Happy individuals are generally more optimistic and resilient in the face of life's challenges. Their collective positivity can help them tackle difficulties together with a sense of determination and confidence.
Happy couples often enjoy spending quality time together. Their shared interests and enjoyment of each other's company create a deeper and more meaningful connection.

Smiling is a simple yet impactful act of kindness. Happy partners are more likely to engage in acts of kindness and thoughtfulness toward each other, nurturing their relationship.

Research has suggested that individuals in happy relationships tend to live longer and enjoy better health. Their shared happiness can contribute to a longer and more fulfilling life together.

When both individuals in a relationship are happy and frequently share smiles, it creates an atmosphere of positivity, mutual support, and effective communication. This, in turn, strengthens the relationship and leads to a more enduring and satisfying connection.

Chapter Seven

Boosts Mood

In the small coastal village of Serenity Bay, nestled between rolling hills and the tranquil sea, there lived a woman named Lila who understood the magical power of smiles in boosting one's mood. Lila had a unique story that revealed how her radiant smile had not only transformed her life but had also become an essential part of the village's way of life.

Lila's story began on a particularly gloomy day. It had been raining for weeks, and the villagers were feeling disheartened. The weight of the relentless gray clouds had cast a shadow over Serenity Bay. Lila, however, refused to be affected by the bleak weather.

As she strolled through the village, she wore a warm, constant smile on her face. She greeted each person she met with a kind word and a bright smile, even in the face of the drenching rain. The villagers were puzzled by Lila's unwavering cheerfulness, but they couldn't help but smile back.

One day, Lila encountered a young girl named Sofia, who was standing by her window, gazing out at the relentless downpour. Lila approached Sofia and said, "Don't let the rain get you down, dear. Let's find a reason to smile even on the rainiest days."

She proceeded to teach Sofia a series of cheerful songs and dances. Together, they created rain-themed artwork, and Lila's smile remained a constant source of joy throughout their activities. By the end of the day, Sofia's mood had been lifted, and the two of them shared a beautiful, shared smile.

Word of Lila's extraordinary ability to boost people's moods through her smile soon spread throughout the village. The villagers realized that her approach was a simple yet powerful way to uplift their spirits, even on the gloomiest days. They embraced the idea and began to smile more frequently.

Over time, Lila's approach to boosting moods through smiles had profound effects:

1. **Emotional Contagion:** Lila's smile was contagious. When she smiled, it inspired those around her to smile back, creating a ripple effect of joy and positivity.

2. **Positive Focus:** Smiles encouraged a positive focus. The act of smiling helped people look for the bright side of life, even in the face of adversity.

3. **Mind-Body Connection:** Lila's smile triggered the release of feel-good hormones, which had a direct impact on mood and emotions.

4. **Improved Relationships:** The village of Serenity Bay became a closer-knit community. Smiles enhanced communication, created a more welcoming atmosphere, and nurtured relationships.

5. **Stress Reduction:** Smiles alleviated stress. By approaching challenges with a smile, villagers were better equipped to manage life's difficulties and maintain a balanced mood.

Serenity Bay soon became known for its cheerful residents, who found reasons to smile even when the sun wasn't shining. The village's transformation from a gloomy place to a beacon of happiness was a testament to the incredible mood-boosting power of smiles.

Lila's story demonstrated that a simple smile had the potential to boost one's mood, inspire others, and transform an entire community's outlook on life. It was a reminder that even on the cloudiest of days, a genuine smile could bring sunshine to the heart.

Smiling triggers the release of endorphins, our brain's natural feel-good chemicals, leading to an instant mood lift Smiling can boost mood due to several interconnected psychological and physiological factors

When you smile, your brain releases a cascade of feel-good neurochemicals called endorphins. These natural opioids act as mood lifters, reducing pain and creating a sense of happiness

Smiling can lead to a decrease in stress-related hormones, such as cortisol.
 This reduction in stress hormones contributes to a more relaxed and positive emotional state

Smiling helps balance the levels of key neurotransmitters in the brain, including dopamine and serotonin, which are associated with feelings of pleasure and well-being.
Smiling can initiate a positive feedback loop
.
 When you smile, your brain perceives it as an expression of happiness, even if it's initially forced. Over time, this can lead to genuine feelings of happiness.

Smiling is a social cue that signals friendliness and approachability.
When others respond positively to your smile, it can create a sense of social connection and boost your mood.

Smiling can trigger physical relaxation, such as a reduction in muscle tension and a lower heart rate, which contributes to a sense of calm and contentment.
Positive emotions associated with smiling can improve cognitive function, problem-solving abilities, and creativity.

Smiling's mood-boosting effects are a result of a complex interplay of biochemical reactions, psychological responses, and their impact on both your body and your interactions with others.
 Even a simple smile can have a significant influence on your overall sense of well-being.

Chapter Eight
Reduces Stress

In the fast-paced and often chaotic city of Stressington, where people were always in a rush, there lived a man named Leo who had a secret to reducing stress. His secret was not a high-tech gadget or an expensive spa treatment; it was simply his ability to smile, even in the most stressful of situations.

Leo had always been a cheerful and optimistic person, even when he faced the overwhelming demands of his job in a busy corporate office. He believed that a smile was a powerful tool for reducing stress, and he had an extraordinary story to prove it.

One particularly challenging day at the office, Leo was bombarded with urgent tasks, deadlines, and a demanding boss who seemed determined to test his limits. As stress levels soared around him, Leo made a conscious decision to smile.

Every time he felt overwhelmed, he would pause and flash a warm, serene smile. It didn't take long for his coworkers to notice. At first, they were puzzled by his apparent calmness amidst the chaos, but they soon found themselves drawn to his positive demeanor.

Over time, Leo's smile became a source of solace and inspiration for his colleagues. They began to emulate his approach, and, to their surprise, found that the simple act of smiling could alleviate their stress as well. It became a sort of unspoken rule in the office: whenever stress levels peaked, it was time to smile.

As Leo continued to embrace the power of smiling in stressful situations, he discovered that smiles had the following effects on stress reduction:

1. **Endorphin Release:** Smiling triggered the release of endorphins, the body's natural mood enhancers. These endorphins counteracted the effects of stress hormones and created a sense of well-being.

2. **Relaxation Response:** Smiles helped activate the body's relaxation response, which lowered heart rate and reduced blood pressure, both of which contributed to stress reduction.

3. **Positive Mindset:** Smiles encouraged a more optimistic mindset. Leo found that approaching challenges with a smile allowed him to see opportunities instead of obstacles.

4. **Improved Communication:** Smiles enhanced communication, making interactions with coworkers more pleasant and collaborative. This led to a reduction in workplace tension and stress.

5. **Resilience:** Smiles helped build emotional resilience. Leo discovered that he could bounce back from setbacks with more ease and confidence when he faced them with a positive outlook.

Stressington soon witnessed a transformation. What was once a city known for its frazzled, overworked residents became a place where people smiled more, even in the face of stress. The city's bustling pace remained, but the smiles had the power to transform the stressful atmosphere into a more balanced and manageable one.

The story of Leo in Stressington served as a reminder that a simple smile could be a powerful tool for reducing stress. It was not just a gesture of happiness but also a strategy for maintaining well-being in the face of life's most demanding challenges.

When you smile, your brain releases endorphins, which are natural feel-good chemicals. These endorphins act as natural painkillers and mood enhancers, reducing the perception of stress and promoting a sense of well-being

Smiling can lead to a decrease in the production of stress-related hormones, particularly cortisol.
High cortisol levels are associated with increased stress and anxiety, so when smiling reduces cortisol, it helps lower overall stress levels

Smiling often involves deep and relaxed breathing, which can increase the flow of oxygen to the brain and body.
This helps to counteract the physiological changes that occur during the body's "fight or flight" stress response

When you smile, your brain interprets this as a signal of happiness, even if the smile is initially forced. This can trigger a positive feedback loop where the brain begins to produce more positive emotions, reducing stress.

Smiling can relax facial muscles, and this relaxation can signal to the brain that you are not under stress. As a result, it can help to lower overall tension in the body.

Smiling is a universal sign of friendliness and approachability. When you smile at others or interact with people who are smiling, it can lead to positive social interactions that reduce stress by providing a sense of connection and support.

When you smile or engage in a pleasant activity, it can serve as a distraction from the stressors in your life, allowing you to momentarily shift your focus away from sources of stress.

Smiling has a direct impact on your mood. Even if you start by forcing a smile, it can eventually lead to genuine positive feelings, further reducing stress.

Smiling can reduce stress by triggering a series of positive psychological and physiological responses that counteract the body's stress response and promote a sense of relaxation and well-being. Incorporating more smiles into your daily life can be a simple yet effective way to manage and reduce stress.

Chapter Nine
Enhances Relationships

In the bustling city of Harmonyville, where people led busy lives and relationships often felt strained, there lived a man named James who understood the profound role of smiles in enhancing relationships. He was known as "Smiling James" throughout the city, and his radiant smile was the cornerstone of his wisdom on the subject.

James had always believed that smiles were more than just gestures of happiness; they were bridges that connected people on a deeper level. His journey to understanding the significance of smiles in relationships began with a chance encounter.

One sunny day, while walking through a crowded park, James saw a woman who appeared distressed, sitting alone on a bench. Her face was etched with worry, and her shoulders slumped under the weight of her concerns. Unable to ignore her obvious distress, James decided to approach her.

With a warm, compassionate smile, James greeted her, "Hello, is everything okay?"

Startled by the unexpected kindness, the woman looked up, and her troubled expression began to soften. James took a seat beside her and, with genuine concern, listened to her story. As they spoke, he maintained his warm smile, offering words of comfort and understanding.

By the end of their conversation, the woman's face had transformed. Her initial distress had faded, replaced by a sense of relief and gratitude. The connection that had formed between them was profound, all thanks to James's simple act of kindness and his warm, genuine smile.

As James continued his journey, he discovered that smiles had a profound effect on enhancing relationships:

1. **Building Trust:** A warm smile was the first step in building trust. It signaled that a person was approachable, kind, and genuine, fostering a sense of trust and openness.

2. **Positive Communication:** Smiles encouraged positive and open communication. When people smiled, it conveyed empathy and encouraged active listening, which was essential for nurturing strong relationships.

3. **Conflict Resolution:** In moments of disagreement, a smile could act as a bridge. Approaching conflicts with a smile often defused tension and made it easier for people to find common ground.

4. **Creating Bonds:** Smiles were the glue that held relationships together. By smiling, individuals not only strengthened existing bonds but also formed new connections.

5. **Acts of Kindness:** Smiles often led to acts of kindness. In Harmonyville, people frequently engaged in friendly exchanges, offered help, and performed random acts of kindness, all inspired by a smile.

James shared his insights with the people of Harmonyville, encouraging them to smile more often and use the power of a smile to enhance their relationships. The city embraced this idea wholeheartedly, and it soon became a place known for its friendly, approachable, and kind-hearted residents.

As the years passed, relationships in Harmonyville deepened and grew stronger. The city was a testament to the power of smiles in enhancing connections, nurturing trust, and fostering a sense of community. The story of Harmonyville served as a reminder that a simple, genuine smile was not just an expression of happiness but also the key to enriching and enhancing the relationships that made life truly meaningful.

Smile is a universal sign of friendliness and approachability, making it easier to connect with others and build positive relationships

Smile is a universal sign of friendliness and approachability.
When you smile, you signal to others that you are open to communication and interaction.
This encourages people to approach you, leading to more opportunities for social connections.

When you meet someone with a smile, it sets a positive tone for the interaction.
First impressions are powerful, and a warm smile can make others feel welcome and appreciated.
Smiling during conversations conveys that you are engaged and interested in what the other person is saying.

This can lead to better communication and understanding between individuals.
Smiles can foster trust and likability. When someone smiles, they are perceived as more trustworthy, and people tend to prefer being around those who appear approachable and pleasant.

Smiling can diffuse tense situations and make it easier to resolve conflicts. When both parties in a disagreement smile, it becomes more likely that they will approach the issue with a positive and cooperative attitude

Smiles are contagious. When you smile at someone, they are more likely to reciprocate with a smile, creating a shared positive emotional experience that strengthens the bond between individuals.

Smiling can create a sense of emotional connection and intimacy. It's a way of expressing warmth and affection, which can deepen relationships with friends, family, and romantic partners.

When you smile at someone, it can help reduce their stress levels. This, in turn, makes the interaction more pleasant and memorable, strengthening the relationship.
Smiling within a group or team can promote a positive and collaborative atmosphere. It fosters a sense of unity and can lead to more effective teamwork.

Smiles are understood and appreciated across cultures, making them a valuable tool for building connections with people from diverse backgrounds\

Smiling serves as a powerful social cue that can enhance relationships by promoting trust, likability, positive interactions, and shared emotional experiences.

Incorporating more smiles into your interactions can lead to stronger, more positive, and more fulfilling relationships with others.

Chapter Ten
Improves Health

In the peaceful village of Serenitown, nestled amidst lush green hills and rolling meadows, there lived a wise old woman named Eliza. She was the village's beloved herbalist, renowned for her knowledge of plants and their healing properties. However, what truly set Eliza apart was her profound belief in the power of smiles to improve health.

Eliza's journey to this realization began during her own struggle with illness. Many years ago, she had faced a debilitating illness that left her bedridden and disheartened. It was a dark and challenging time, and she had almost given up hope.

One evening, as she lay in her dimly lit room, her granddaughter, Sarah, visited her. She was a bright and cheerful child who had inherited her grandmother's warm smile. Sarah sat by Eliza's bedside and shared stories, told jokes, and made funny faces to lift her spirits. Despite her illness, Eliza couldn't help but smile at Sarah's antics.

To her surprise, Eliza noticed a slight improvement in her condition the following day. Her body felt a little lighter, and her heart a little happier. Eliza began to observe how even the brief moments of laughter and smiles she shared with Sarah seemed to alleviate her pain and discomfort.

Inspired by this change, Eliza decided to dedicate herself to the study of the connection between smiles and health. She found that her experiences were not unique; there was scientific evidence that supported her observations:

1. **Endorphin Release:** Smiling triggered the release of endorphins, the body's natural feel-good chemicals. These endorphins acted as natural painkillers, reducing discomfort and boosting mood.

2. **Stress Reduction:** Smiles helped reduce the levels of stress hormones in the body. Lower stress levels were linked to better immune system function and overall health.

3. **Immune System Boost:** The positive emotions associated with smiling enhanced the immune system, making the body better equipped to fend off illnesses and infections.

4. **Cardiovascular Benefits:** Smiling was associated with improved cardiovascular health. It lowered blood pressure, reduced heart rate, and decreased the risk of heart-related issues.

5. **Longevity:** Studies suggested that those who smiled more frequently tended to live longer and healthier lives, possibly due to the positive impact on overall well-being.

Eliza shared her findings with the people of Serenitown, encouraging them to incorporate more smiles into their daily lives. The village embraced the idea wholeheartedly and began to smile at one another with greater frequency. The community grew more connected, happier, and, most importantly, healthier.

As the years passed, the health benefits of smiles became more apparent in Serenitown. People reported fewer illnesses, aches, and pains. The village became known for its warm and cheerful atmosphere, and travelers from neighboring towns visited to experience the magic of Serenitown's health-improving smiles.

Eliza's journey had not only transformed her own life but also the lives of everyone in Serenitown. The story of Serenitown stands as a testament to the incredible healing power of smiles, a reminder that the simple act of smiling can bring about not only happiness but also improved health and well-being.

 Research suggests that smiling may boost the immune system, reduce pain, and lower blood pressure, contributing to better overall health

When you smile, your brain releases endorphins, which are natural mood lifters. These endorphins reduce stress hormones, such as cortisol, helping to lower overall stress levels and promote a sense of relaxation.

Endorphins released when you smile can act as natural painkillers. They can help reduce pain and discomfort, making you feel more comfortable and at ease.

Smiling can lead to a decrease in blood pressure, promoting cardiovascular health. Reduced blood pressure can lower the risk of heart disease and other related health issues.

The positive emotions associated with smiling can boost the immune system. A stronger immune system helps your body defend against illnesses and infections more effectively.

Smiling is linked to an improved mood and a more positive outlook on life. A positive attitude is associated with better mental health and resilience in the face of life's challenges.

Smiling can increase your pain tolerance, making you better equipped to deal with discomfort or painful situations.

Smiling often involves relaxed facial muscles, which can send signals to your brain that you are not under stress. This physical relaxation contributes to an overall sense of calm and well-being.
Positive emotions from smiling can improve cognitive functions like problem-solving, creativity, and decision-making.
Some studies have suggested that people with a more positive outlook on life, often reflected by smiling, tend to live longer and enjoy better overall health.

Positive interactions resulting from smiling can lead to stronger social connections, reducing feelings of loneliness and promoting mental well-being.

Smiling can have a profound impact on your physical and mental health. It can reduce stress, improve mood, strengthen the immune system, and even promote cardiovascular health.
It's a simple and effective way to contribute to your overall well-being.

Chapter Eleven
Lifts Others' Spirits

In the charming town of Harmonyville, there lived a woman named Grace who had an extraordinary gift: her smile had the power to lift the spirits of those around her. She understood the profound impact her smile had on others and used it as a force for good.

Grace's story began during her childhood when she faced a particularly challenging time. She lost her father in a tragic accident, and the weight of grief cast a shadow over her life. As she navigated her way through the darkness, Grace noticed the positive effect a simple smile from a stranger or friend could have on her mood. She realized that a smile could be a lifeline, pulling her out of despair and into the light.

Years passed, and Grace made it her mission to share the joy she had found through the power of her own smile. She believed that by uplifting others' spirits, she could make the world a brighter place.

One sunny day, as Grace strolled through the town park, she encountered a despondent young boy named Sam, sitting alone on a bench with his head hung low.

Grace approached Sam, her smile radiating warmth. "Hi there," she greeted him with a friendly tone.

Sam looked up, his eyes filled with sadness. But as he met Grace's gaze and her beaming smile, he couldn't help but smile back, if only for a moment. Grace sat down beside him, and they began to chat. She shared stories, listened to his concerns, and offered words of encouragement.

With each passing moment, Sam's spirits started to lift. Her kindness and her smile had transformed his day from one of sorrow to one of hope. Sam left the park that day with a renewed sense of optimism.

Grace continued to spread her uplifting smiles throughout Harmonyville. Her reputation as a "Smile Ambassador" grew, and she became a cherished figure in the community.

She found that her ability to lift others' spirits was not only an act of kindness but also had a ripple effect:

1. **Positivity Multiplier:** Grace's smile was infectious, brightening the mood of those she encountered. When people received her warm smile, they were more inclined to smile at others, creating a chain reaction of positivity.

2. **Building Connection:** Grace's genuine smile built bridges of connection with people from all walks of life. It fostered a sense of community and camaraderie within Harmonyville.

3. **Stress Relief:** Grace's smile acted as a natural stress reliever. When people were feeling overwhelmed or anxious, her presence and smile provided a calming influence, lifting their spirits.

4. **Acts of Kindness:** Grace's uplifting smile often inspired people to perform random acts of kindness for others, creating a compassionate and supportive environment.

5. **Improved Well-Being:** Through her mission to lift others' spirits, Grace found that her own well-being improved as well. Her happiness and fulfillment grew as she saw the positive impact she had on her community.

As time passed, Harmonyville lived up to its name, becoming a place where people not only smiled more but also actively sought to lift the spirits of those around them. The town thrived on the principle that small acts of kindness, like Grace's uplifting smile, could make a significant difference in the lives of its residents.

Grace's journey in Harmonyville was a testament to the incredible power of a simple smile to lift others' spirits and create a more harmonious and joyful world. It reminded everyone that a warm, genuine smile could be the light that guides someone out of darkness and into the sun.

Smiles are contagious, and by smiling, you can brighten someone else's day, creating a ripple effect of positivity.
Emotions are contagious, and people tend to mirror the emotional expressions of those around them. When you smile, others are more likely to experience an uplift in their own mood.

A smile is a universal sign of friendliness and approachability. When you smile at someone, it signals that you are open to interaction and that you value their presence. This creates a positive and welcoming atmosphere.

Your smile can encourage others to respond with their own positive emotions. This positive feedback loop can lead to an overall improvement in everyone's mood.

Smiling can trigger the release of endorphins and reduce stress hormones, which can lead to a sense of relaxation and well-being in those around you.

Seeing someone smile can foster feelings of empathy and understanding. It can make people feel like they are seen and appreciated, which can be especially important during difficult times.

When someone smiles at you, it can boost your self-esteem and confidence. This can be particularly helpful in encouraging others to tackle challenges or try new things.
Smiling is an excellent way to break the ice in social situations. It makes others feel more comfortable and encourages them to engage in conversation and positive interactions.

Smiling can create a more cooperative and harmonious environment. People are more likely to work together and be willing to compromise when they feel positive and supported.

In potentially tense or awkward situations, a smile can ease tension and promote a sense of calm. It can make difficult conversations more approachable and less confrontational.
A simple smile is a small act of kindness that costs nothing but can have a significant impact on someone's day. It shows that you care and that you want to contribute to their well-being.

Smiling has a ripple effect on the emotional state of those around you. It can create a more positive, friendly, and supportive atmosphere, lifting the spirits of others and contributing to improved social interactions and overall well-being.

Chapter Twelve

Increases Confidence

In a bustling city named Confidenceville, there lived a young woman named Sarah who was known for her unwavering confidence. Sarah had a secret weapon that she carried with her at all times – her smile. She believed that her radiant smile held the key to increasing her confidence.

Sarah had not always been this self-assured. In her youth, she had struggled with self-esteem and shyness. She often felt invisible in a sea of people and found it challenging to express herself. It wasn't until one fateful day that she discovered the incredible power of her smile.

One sunny afternoon, Sarah had an important job interview for a position she had dreamed of her entire life. She had spent weeks preparing for it, but anxiety gnawed at her. As she walked to the interview location, she noticed her reflection in a storefront window. Her face was tense and devoid of its usual warmth.

At that moment, Sarah decided to try something different. She forced herself to smile, believing that it might boost her confidence. She smiled at the passerby on the street, the friendly cashier at the coffee shop, and even the pigeons in the park. With each smile, she felt a bit more relaxed and a little more confident.

By the time she arrived at the interview, she was greeted with a warm smile from the receptionist. Sarah's newfound confidence allowed her to express herself with ease during the interview. She answered questions with poise, maintained eye contact, and showcased her skills and qualifications. Her smile was her secret weapon, boosting her self-assurance as well as making a lasting impression.

Sarah was offered the job, and as she left the building, she realized the incredible transformation that had taken place. Her smile had not only won her the job but had also ignited a spark of confidence within her.

Emboldened by her newfound realization, Sarah continued to use her smile as a tool to increase her confidence in various aspects of her life. She discovered that smiling had a profound impact on her self-esteem, and here's how:

1. **Positive Feedback Loop:** Sarah's smile created a positive feedback loop. When she smiled, people responded positively to her, which, in turn, boosted her self-esteem and made her feel more confident.

2. **Stress Reduction:** Smiling helped Sarah combat anxiety and stress. When she faced challenging situations, her smile acted as a natural stress reliever, allowing her to approach them with more confidence.

3. **Improved Social Skills:** Sarah's smile made her more approachable and open to social interactions. This improved her social skills, and the positive feedback she received from others further increased her self-assurance.

4. **Optimistic Mindset:** Smiling encouraged Sarah to maintain a more optimistic mindset. She began to see opportunities instead of obstacles, which boosted her confidence in her abilities to overcome challenges.

5. **Charisma and Attraction:** Sarah's confidence and the positive energy she exuded through her smile made her more charismatic and attractive to others, further boosting her self-esteem.

Over time, Sarah became a well-known figure in Confidenceville, not just for her radiant smile but for the unshakable self-confidence that she radiated. She shared her secret with others, inspiring them to smile more and harness the incredible power of a smile to boost their own confidence.

The story of Sarah in Confidenceville taught everyone that a genuine, warm smile could transform not only how others perceived you but also how you perceived yourself. It was a reminder that confidence often begins with a smile.

When you smile, you are more likely to see yourself in a positive light. It can enhance your self-esteem and help you feel better about your appearance and the way you present yourself to the world.

Smiling triggers the release of endorphins, which are natural mood boosters. The positive emotions associated with smiling can lead to a more optimistic outlook on life and an increased sense of confidence.

Smiling can lower stress levels by decreasing the release of stress hormones, such as cortisol. With lower stress and anxiety, you are better equipped to handle challenges and approach new situations with confidence.

A smiling individual is often seen as more approachable and friendly, making it easier for others to interact with you. Positive social interactions can boost your self-assurance.

Smiling can make you appear more open and engaging in conversations. This can lead to better communication with others and increase your confidence in social situations. The more you smile, the more you may receive positive responses from others.

These responses can reinforce your self-confidence and encourage you to continue smiling.

When you meet people with a smile, it sets a positive tone for the interaction. This can lead to better first impressions, enhancing your confidence in social and professional settings.

A smile can signal to others that you are comfortable and self-assured. It can boost your assertiveness, making it easier to express your thoughts and ideas.

Smiling is a form of positive body language.

It can help convey confidence and enthusiasm, which are important nonverbal cues in various situations.

Smiling individuals are often more optimistic when facing challenges. This optimism can boost your problem-solving abilities and confidence in your problem-solving skills.

Smiling has the power to boost self-confidence by improving your self-image, reducing stress and anxiety, and enhancing your interactions with others.

It can lead to a more positive and confident outlook on life and your abilities, making it easier to navigate both personal and professional situations with assurance.

Chapter Thirteen
Radiates Happiness

In the picturesque village of Sunflower Valley, there lived a woman named Lily who was known for her remarkable ability to radiate happiness. From her sparkling eyes to her ever-present smile, Lily seemed to exude an aura of positivity that touched the hearts of everyone she met.

Lily's reputation for spreading happiness had grown far and wide. People from neighboring villages would visit Sunflower Valley just to bask in her radiant presence. However, no one truly knew the source of Lily's boundless joy.

One bright morning, a young girl named Mia arrived in Sunflower Valley. Mia had been struggling with a heavy heart due to various challenges in her life. She had heard about Lily's extraordinary ability to radiate happiness and decided to seek her out in the hopes of finding a solution to her own unhappiness.

Mia found Lily tending to her colorful garden, the very sight of which brought a smile to Mia's face. She approached Lily and, with a touch of awe, said, "I've heard about your incredible ability to radiate happiness. I'm desperately in need of some happiness in my life. Can you help me, Lily?"

Lily turned toward Mia, her warm eyes twinkling. "Of course, dear. But first, I need to share my story with you."

She led Mia to a cozy spot in her garden and began to speak.

"Years ago, I, too, faced a time when my life felt empty and devoid of happiness. I had lost my job, my home, and even my sense of purpose. It was during this dark period that I stumbled upon a dusty old journal in the attic of my new home. As I leafed through its pages, I found a record of the garden's creation by a previous owner. It was filled with sketches, notes, and observations about the plants, flowers, and animals that once thrived here."

Lily paused and took a deep breath, her gaze filled with nostalgia.

"I decided to restore this garden to its former glory. I began planting, tending, and nurturing each flower and tree, just as the journal's author had done. The process of watching the garden come to life filled me with an inexplicable sense of purpose and joy. I discovered that by caring for the garden, I was also caring for my own well-being."

Mia listened intently, captivated by Lily's story.

"Over time," Lily continued, "I realized that happiness isn't something you can chase. It's something you create. Just like this garden, we must cultivate and nurture happiness in our lives. The more you invest in positive thoughts, kindness, and gratitude, the more you radiate happiness."

Inspired by Lily's tale, Mia decided to stay in Sunflower Valley for a while. She joined Lily in the garden, learning to care for the flowers and connect with nature. As she embraced these practices, Mia began to feel a transformation within herself. Her heavy heart gradually lightened, and a smile started to blossom on her face.

In time, Mia, too, became a beacon of happiness in Sunflower Valley. Her newfound joy and optimism were infectious, touching the lives of those around her, just as Lily had done for her.

Sunflower Valley, already a place of natural beauty, became even more enchanting with the addition of Lily and Mia's radiant happiness. The village was not only blessed with a breathtaking garden but also with the warmth of two souls who had discovered the secret to radiating happiness through the simple act of nurturing positivity and sharing it with the world.

Smiling is a universal sign of happiness. When you smile, it conveys to others that you are feeling joyful and content, creating a visible and contagious display of happiness.
Happiness is contagious, and when you smile, it encourages others to mirror your positive emotions.
This creates a ripple effect where your happiness can brighten the mood of those you interact with.

Smiles promote shared positive experiences. When you and others exchange smiles, it fosters a sense of connection and shared happiness, reinforcing the feeling of joy.
Smiling in the company of others strengthens bonds and encourages positive social interactions.

It can make your relationships more enjoyable and fulfilling. Smiling triggers the release of endorphins, which act as natural mood lifters. These endorphins can reduce stress and anxiety, contributing to a greater sense of happiness.

The act of smiling itself can improve your mood. Even if you start with a forced smile, it can eventually lead to genuine feelings of happiness, creating a feedback loop of positivity.

Smiling is often associated with a more optimistic outlook on life. People who smile frequently tend to have a more positive perspective and a greater sense of happiness.
When you smile, you appear more confident and approachable.

This positive self-presentation can lead to increased self-assuredness and happiness.
Smiling contributes to your overall well-being by reducing stress, improving relationships, and enhancing your mood, which, in turn, promotes greater happiness.

A simple smile is a small act of kindness that can brighten someone else's day, making both you and the recipient happier. This reinforces the cycle of happiness.

Smiling radiates happiness by expressing your joy, triggering positive emotions in others, enhancing your relationships, and contributing to your overall well-being.

It is a simple yet powerful way to spread and experience happiness in your life.

Chapter Fourteen
The Science of Smiles

Once upon a time in the small town of Graceton, there lived a young girl named Emma who was known for her perpetual smile. Emma's smile was infectious, spreading warmth and happiness wherever she went. Her smile was so remarkable that it had caught the attention of a curious scientist, Dr. Benjamin Clarke, who was visiting Graceton to study the science of smiles.

Dr. Clarke was a psychologist with a passion for understanding human behavior. He had heard about Emma's extraordinary smile and believed it could hold the key to unlocking the secrets of happiness. Determined to unravel the mystery of her perpetual cheerfulness, he approached Emma one sunny afternoon in the town square.

"Hello, Emma," Dr. Clarke greeted her with a friendly smile of his own.

"Hi there!" Emma beamed back, her eyes twinkling with joy. "What can I do for you, Dr. Clarke?"

"I've heard about your amazing smile, and I'm conducting a study on the science of smiles. I was wondering if you'd be willing to participate," Dr. Clarke explained.

Emma's face lit up even more. "Of course! I'd love to help."

Over the following weeks, Dr. Clarke observed Emma's daily life, interviewed her friends and family, and conducted various tests and surveys. He soon discovered that Emma's smile was not just a random occurrence but a result of several factors:

1. Positive Outlook: Emma had a naturally optimistic view of the world. She focused on the good in people and situations, which contributed to her overall happiness.

2. Acts of Kindness: Emma was actively involved in helping others in her community. Whether it was volunteering at the local shelter, assisting the elderly, or simply offering a friendly ear, she found joy in making a difference in people's lives.

3. Strong Social Connections: Emma had a vast network of friends and loved ones. Her close relationships provided emotional support and a sense of belonging, which contributed to her happiness.

4. Resilience: Emma faced life's challenges with a smile. She didn't let setbacks bring her down, instead viewing them as opportunities for growth.

5. Physical Health: Emma took care of her physical well-being through regular exercise and a healthy diet, which enhanced her overall happiness and well-being.

As Dr. Clarke gathered this data, he realized that Emma's smile wasn't just a result of happiness; it was also a driver of happiness in her life and the lives of those around her.

With this newfound understanding, Dr. Clarke created a program that incorporated Emma's principles into a series of workshops for the people of Graceton. He taught them the significance of positivity, kindness, social connections, resilience, and physical health in achieving a happier life. The town embraced these teachings, and slowly but surely, a ripple effect of smiles and happiness began to spread throughout Graceton.

Over time, the town transformed into a place where people smiled more, shared kindness, and built stronger relationships. Graceton became known as the "Town of Smiles," attracting visitors from all over who wanted to experience the science of smiles for themselves.

Emma, the girl with the infectious smile, continued to brighten the town with her joy. She was not just the catalyst for Dr. Clarke's scientific study but also the embodiment of its findings. Graceton, once an ordinary town, had become a beacon of happiness and positivity, all thanks to the simple yet profound science of smiles.

Chapter Fifteen
The Social Significance of Smiles

In the vibrant city of Unityville, people understood the immense social significance of smiles. It was a place where smiles were not just expressions of happiness but also tools for building connections and fostering a strong sense of community.

One of the key advocates for the power of smiles in Unityville was a woman named Emily. She had spent years studying the impact of smiles on social interactions and had become a true expert on the subject. Emily believed that smiles were the universal language of friendship and compassion.

Emily's story began with a simple act of kindness. One rainy day, she was waiting at a bus stop when a stranger approached. He was drenched from head to toe, carrying a broken umbrella. His disheartened expression conveyed frustration and sadness. Emily, without hesitation, flashed a warm and welcoming smile. In response, the stranger's face slowly brightened, and he couldn't help but smile back.

From that moment, Emily realized the profound impact a smile could have on people's emotions and social connections. She became determined to use smiles as a tool for creating a more connected and compassionate society.

As Emily delved deeper into her research, she discovered the various ways smiles had social significance:

1. **Friendship:** A smile was the first step in forming new friendships. It communicated openness, warmth, and approachability, which made it easier for people to initiate conversations and build bonds.

2. **Trust:** Smiles were seen as indicators of trustworthiness. When people smiled, they were perceived as more reliable and honest, which was essential in forming lasting relationships.

3. **Conflict Resolution:** In times of disagreement and conflict, a smile could serve as an olive branch. Emily found that approaching disputes with a smile diffused tension and made it easier for people to find common ground.

4. **Communication:** Smiles enhanced communication. A smile conveyed empathy and encouraged active listening, making conversations more meaningful and satisfying.

5. **Acts of Kindness:** Smiles often led to acts of kindness. In Unityville, people frequently engaged in friendly exchanges, helping one another, and performing random acts of kindness, all triggered by a smile.

6. **Strengthening Community:** Unityville was a tight-knit community, thanks to the importance placed on smiles. People felt a sense of belonging, trust, and mutual support, which contributed to the town's harmonious atmosphere.

As Emily shared her findings and her passion for the social significance of smiles, Unityville embraced the idea wholeheartedly. It became a place where people actively smiled at one another, not just as a sign of happiness but as an acknowledgment of shared humanity and community.

Unityville's story serves as a reminder of the profound social significance of smiles. In a world where divisions and conflicts often overshadow unity, the power of a simple smile has the potential to bridge gaps, foster trust, and strengthen the bonds that connect us all. It is a testament to the idea that smiles are not just expressions of personal happiness but also the foundation of a more empathetic and harmonious society.

Chapter Sixteen
Overcoming Obstacles to Smiling

In the vibrant city of New Horizons, where dreams and ambitions flourished, there lived a young woman named Sarah. Sarah had always believed in the power of a smile, but her journey was marked by a unique obstacle that tested her unwavering commitment to happiness. Her story was one of overcoming obstacles to smiling.

Sarah had a deep passion for music and had dreamed of becoming a professional singer from a young age. Her journey in pursuit of her dream was filled with ups and downs, but she faced her biggest obstacle when she was involved in a car accident that left her with a permanent scar on her right cheek. The scar was a constant reminder of the accident and had made Sarah self-conscious about her appearance.

Sarah's scar wasn't just physical; it affected her emotionally. She withdrew from the music scene, feeling that her dreams were shattered. The spotlight had been her comfort zone, but now she felt exposed and vulnerable. Her confidence had taken a hit, and her radiant smile was replaced by a guarded expression.

One evening, while sitting in her dimly lit apartment, Sarah received an unexpected phone call from a friend named Max, a talented pianist and songwriter. Max had heard about her accident and the emotional struggles she was facing. He offered to collaborate on a new song that he believed would help her regain her confidence and overcome the obstacles to smiling.

The song, aptly titled "Unscarred Melodies," was a poignant ballad that celebrated the beauty in imperfections and the power of resilience. Max's heartfelt lyrics and Sarah's soulful voice conveyed the message that scars, both physical and emotional, were a testament to the battles one had faced and the strength one had gained.

As they worked on the song, Sarah realized that she had been looking at her scar the wrong way. It wasn't a mark of imperfection but a symbol of her strength and survival. It was a part of her story, and she needed to embrace it with the same passion she had for her music.

With "Unscarred Melodies" completed, Sarah felt a renewed sense of purpose. She decided to step back into the spotlight and perform the song at a local music event. When she stepped onto the stage, she was met with an enthusiastic crowd that cheered her on. Sarah looked out at the audience, and for the first time in a long while, her radiant smile returned.

Sarah's journey taught her several valuable lessons about overcoming obstacles to smiling:

1. **Self-Acceptance:** Sarah realized that self-acceptance was crucial. Embracing her scar was the first step toward regaining her confidence.

2. **Resilience:** Her experience highlighted the power of resilience. Life's obstacles could be overcome with determination and a positive mindset.

3. **Supportive Relationships:** Max's support was instrumental in her journey. Surrounding herself with supportive friends and collaborators was crucial to her success.

Sarah's triumphant return to the world of music and her smile's reappearance marked a significant chapter in her life. Her story celebrated the idea that smiles could be rediscovered, even in the face of life's most daunting challenges. It was a testament to the power of perseverance, self-acceptance, and the unwavering belief in the beauty of imperfections.

Chapter Seventeen
The Art of Smiling: Tips and Techniques

In the heart of the bustling metropolis of Harmonyville, where the pace of life was rapid and the people were always on the move, there was a unique place known as the "Smile Studio." It was a sanctuary for those seeking to master the art of smiling, offering tips and techniques to enhance the joy in their lives.

At the helm of the Smile Studio was a woman named Grace. Grace was not just a smile enthusiast; she was a connoisseur of the art of smiling. Her journey to creating the Smile Studio began with a simple realization: smiles had the power to transform lives, and she wanted to share that magic with the world.

Grace's story was a testament to the idea that a smile was not just an expression of joy but a craft that could be cultivated and perfected. She had always been fascinated by the science behind smiles and the impact they had on individuals and the world. Her journey started with a smile, and her dream was to inspire many more.

At the Smile Studio, Grace offered a comprehensive curriculum for those interested in the art of smiling:

Lesson 1: The Anatomy of a Smile - Grace taught her students the basics, from the muscles involved in smiling to the different types of smiles, including the genuine, the polite, and the sly.

Lesson 2: The Power of Positive Thought - Grace explained that smiling began in the mind. She taught techniques for cultivating a positive mindset and maintaining optimism.

Lesson 3: Smile Practices - Students learned the power of daily smile practices. These included keeping a smile journal, setting smile reminders, and practicing random acts of kindness to generate smiles.

Lesson 4: Smiling in the Mirror - Grace encouraged self-reflection through mirror exercises. She believed that practicing your smile in front of a mirror could help improve your overall demeanor.

Lesson 5: The Science of Smiles - Grace delved into the science behind smiles, including the release of endorphins, stress reduction, and the enhancement of social bonds through smiling.

Lesson 6: The Impact on Others - Students learned about the ripple effect of a smile. Grace taught that a single smile could brighten someone's day and encourage them to pass it on.

Over time, the Smile Studio transformed the lives of its students. They went on to become ambassadors of smiles, radiating positivity and joy wherever they went. The techniques and tips they had learned became a part of their daily routines, and they understood that the art of smiling was not just a personal skill but a gift to the world.

Grace's journey and the success of the Smile Studio reminded people that the art of smiling was more than just a pleasant expression; it was a craft that could be mastered. It was a testament to the power of positive thought, practice, and the incredible impact a simple smile could have on one's life and the lives of those around them.

Chapter Eighteen
The Future of Smiles

In the not-so-distant future, the concept of smiles had evolved into something truly remarkable. In the bustling city of Tomorrowville, technological advancements and a deeper understanding of human emotions had given birth to a whole new dimension of smiles and their role in society. This was the future of smiles.

In Tomorrowville, a young woman named Amelia was at the forefront of this groundbreaking transformation. She had always been fascinated by the emotional power of smiles and had devoted her life to exploring how technology could enhance and harness this power.

Amelia's journey began when she joined an innovative research institute known as the "Center for Emotional Enhancement." This institution was on a mission to redefine human interactions and emotional experiences through technology.

The key discovery that sparked the future of smiles was the development of "Neuro-Smile Enhancers" (NSEs). These were advanced wearable devices that could detect and amplify the emotions associated with smiles. NSEs monitored brain activity, heart rate, and facial expressions, and when they detected a genuine smile, they enhanced it to create an even more positive emotional impact.

The future of smiles had several key features:

1. **Enhanced Communication:** NSEs allowed people to communicate with a greater depth of emotion. When you smiled at someone while wearing an NSE, they could feel your happiness on a much more profound level.

2. **Emotional Telepathy:** With NSEs, people could share their emotions with loved ones across great distances. It was as if they were experiencing the same joy, even if they were miles apart.

3. **Emotion-Sharing Networks:** The development of global emotion-sharing networks allowed people to connect on an emotional level regardless of their physical location. They could send smiles, share happiness, and support one another with incredible ease.

4. **Personal Growth:** NSEs also acted as personal development tools. They provided feedback on the emotional impact of your smiles, helping you understand how to convey positive emotions more effectively.

Amelia's journey to shaping the future of smiles was filled with exciting challenges and discoveries. She worked tirelessly to ensure that this technological evolution did not replace the authenticity of human emotions but rather complemented and enriched them.

The future of smiles was a testament to humanity's unending quest for deeper connections and the profound impact of positive emotions. In Tomorrowville, people had found a way to magnify the power of their smiles, to share happiness and empathy with a level of depth and breadth that was previously unimaginable. It was a bright and hopeful future where smiles played a central role in shaping a better world for all.

Chapter Nineteen

Smiles and Your Well-Being

In the tranquil town of Serenity Springs, nestled amidst lush forests and crystal-clear lakes, the residents had always understood the profound connection between smiles and their well-being. This was a place where the pursuit of happiness was not just a desire but a way of life, and the town's story was a testament to the importance of smiles in nurturing well-being.

At the heart of Serenity Springs lived a wise elder named Oliver. Oliver had dedicated his life to studying the relationship between smiles and well-being. He believed that a genuine smile had the power to transform an individual's health, both physical and mental.

Oliver's journey began with a personal experience. He had faced a period of profound sadness and despair after losing a dear friend. During that difficult time, he had found solace in the smiles and laughter of his community. It was the warm embraces and joyful expressions of his neighbors that had helped him heal.

As he delved deeper into the connection between smiles and well-being, Oliver discovered a wealth of wisdom:

1. **Endorphin Release:** Smiles triggered the release of endorphins, the body's natural mood elevators. This hormone not only improved mood but also had a direct impact on physical well-being.

2. **Stress Reduction:** Smiles were natural stress-relievers. They reduced stress hormones and promoted relaxation, leading to better mental and physical health.

3. **Strong Social Bonds:** Smiles built strong social bonds. In Serenity Springs, close-knit relationships were essential for emotional well-being, and smiles played a key role in creating these connections.

4. **Positive Outlook:** Smiles fostered a positive outlook on life. People who smiled regularly were more optimistic, resilient, and better equipped to handle life's challenges.

5. **Acts of Kindness:** Oliver discovered that smiles inspired acts of kindness. Residents often went out of their way to support one another, creating a cycle of shared happiness and well-being.

As Oliver shared his knowledge with the residents of Serenity Springs, the town embraced the idea that well-being was not just the absence of illness but a state of happiness and contentment. They understood that a genuine, warm smile was not only an expression of personal joy but also a reflection of an individual's commitment to their own well-being.

Serenity Springs became a haven of well-being, where smiles were not just expressions of happiness but also a vital component of a person's physical and mental health. It was a place where smiles nurtured well-being, and the residents celebrated the idea that a simple smile had the power to create a healthier, happier, and more contented life for all.

Chapter Twenty

Smiles in the Workplace

In the heart of the bustling city of Progressville, where ambition and innovation thrived, a remarkable transformation was taking place in the workplace. It was a story of "Smiles in the Workplace," and it showcased the profound impact that a positive and inclusive work environment, fueled by smiles, could have on both employees and the company's success.

Progressville was known for its cutting-edge technology companies, and one of the most prominent among them was InnovateTech Inc. At the helm of InnovateTech was its visionary CEO, Maya. She believed that a smile wasn't just an expression of happiness; it was a catalyst for success.

Maya's journey began when she took over as CEO of InnovateTech. She observed that the corporate culture was suffering from stress and a lack of camaraderie. Employees were working long hours, and the workplace had become a breeding ground for exhaustion and burnout.

Maya understood that to foster innovation and drive success, she needed to create an environment where her employees could thrive. She believed that smiles were the key to building a positive and productive workplace. Here's how she transformed InnovateTech:

1. Smiles as a Daily Ritual: Maya introduced a "Morning Smile" routine. At the start of each day, employees gathered to share a smile and a positive thought, setting a cheerful tone for the day.

2. Recognition and Appreciation: InnovateTech implemented a peer recognition program where employees could nominate their colleagues for their efforts and achievements. Recognized employees received a "Smile of Appreciation" award.

3. Employee Wellness: The company invested in wellness programs, including mindfulness and stress management workshops, to support the mental and physical well-being of its employees.

4. Celebrating Milestones: InnovateTech celebrated both professional and personal milestones with smiles. Whether it was a work anniversary or a new baby, they took the time to acknowledge and celebrate.

5. Inclusive Culture: The company promoted an inclusive culture where all employees felt valued and respected. The open and positive environment encouraged everyone to contribute their best.

The transformation in the workplace was nothing short of remarkable. Employees at InnovateTech were happier, more engaged, and motivated to excel. The positive work culture that Maya had nurtured led to several notable outcomes:

Increased Productivity: The company's productivity soared as employees were more motivated and dedicated to their work.

Innovation: A more relaxed and inclusive work environment fueled creativity and innovation.

Better Retention: The company experienced lower turnover rates as employees felt a deep sense of belonging and satisfaction.

Improved Employee Health: The focus on employee well-being reduced stress levels and led to better physical and mental health.

Maya's story in Progressville was a testament to the power of smiles in the workplace. It was a reminder that a positive and inclusive work culture, fueled by genuine smiles, not only improved employee well-being but also had a direct impact on a company's success. It proved that a happy workplace was not just a dream but a reality worth pursuing for the benefit of all.

Chapter Twenty one
Smiles and Personal Growth

In the serene village of Tranquil Heights, nestled amid rolling hills and lush forests, the residents believed in the transformative power of smiles and their role in personal growth. This was a place where happiness and self-improvement were intricately connected, and the village's story was a testament to the profound impact of smiles on individual development.

At the heart of Tranquil Heights lived a woman named Ella. Ella had always been fascinated by the potential for personal growth and believed that smiles played a central role in this journey. Her own life had been marked by a deep transformation that began with a simple realization: her smile was a reflection of her inner self.

Ella's journey began when she faced a challenging period in her life. She had lost her job, and her self-esteem had hit rock bottom. She often wore a frown on her face, believing that the world was against her. But then, she encountered a kind and wise mentor in Tranquil Heights, an elderly woman named Sophie.

Sophie, too, had experienced her share of hardships, but she had learned the profound significance of personal growth and smiles. She shared with Ella the idea that one's smile was not just an expression of joy but also a mirror to their inner self. Sophie explained that a genuine smile could help transform negative emotions and nurture personal growth.

Ella embarked on a journey to understand and apply this wisdom. She discovered several key lessons about smiles and personal growth:

1. **Mindset Shift:** Ella realized that personal growth began with a shift in mindset. By choosing to see the positive aspects of her life, she could cultivate a more positive outlook.

2. **Smile Practice:** Ella adopted a daily smile practice. She made it a habit to smile at herself in the mirror each morning, reinforcing a positive self-image.

3. **Acts of Kindness:** Ella understood that performing acts of kindness not only brightened the days of others but also brought a sense of fulfillment and personal growth.

4. **Conflict Resolution:** When faced with conflicts, Ella approached them with a smile. She found that a warm smile could defuse tension and foster understanding.

5. **Self-Compassion:** Ella learned to be more compassionate toward herself. She understood that self-improvement required self-acceptance and love.

Over time, Ella's transformation became evident. She not only found a new job but also a deep sense of self-fulfillment and personal growth. Her smiles were no longer a facade but a genuine reflection of her inner peace and happiness.

Ella's journey in Tranquil Heights was a reminder to the world that personal growth and smiles were deeply interconnected. It was a testament to the idea that the key to self-improvement often lay in the simplest of actions – a genuine smile that could transform not just the way one felt but also their outlook on life. It was a journey that celebrated the profound impact of smiles on personal growth and well-being.

Chapter Twenty two

Acts of Kindness: Smiling Beyond Yourself

In the charming town of Kindsville, nestled amidst rolling hills and quaint cottages, the residents had long understood the significance of acts of kindness, especially when it came to smiling beyond themselves. This was a place where generosity and goodwill thrived, and the town's story was a testament to the remarkable ripple effect of kindness and smiles.

At the heart of Kindsville was a woman named Emily. Emily had always been known for her warm smile and her willingness to go above and beyond to help others. Her journey to understanding the power of acts of kindness and smiles began during a particularly challenging period in her life.

Emily had been dealing with her own personal struggles when a kind stranger extended a hand of support and a bright, genuine smile. The stranger's act of kindness and the warmth in their eyes had made all the difference in Emily's life. She had been deeply moved and inspired to pay that kindness forward.

Emily's journey to embracing acts of kindness and spreading smiles was marked by several key moments:

1. **The Power of Small Gestures:** Emily learned that acts of kindness need not be grand or extravagant. Small gestures, like holding a door open, helping with groceries, or offering a sincere compliment, could have a profound impact.

2. **The Ripple Effect:** As Emily extended her kindness to others, she began to see the ripple effect it had on her community. People she had helped often went on to help others, creating a chain of goodwill and positivity.

3. **Smiles as a Universal Language:** Emily understood that a smile was a universal language of kindness. It transcended barriers of language and culture, conveying warmth and empathy to all.

4. **Shared Happiness:** Acts of kindness not only brought joy to others but also filled Emily's heart with happiness. She felt a deep sense of fulfillment in knowing that she could make a positive difference in someone's day.

5. **Creating a Caring Community:** Kindsville became a place where acts of kindness were a way of life. The town was known for its compassionate residents who consistently extended their support to those in need.

Over time, Emily's efforts and those of her fellow townspeople transformed Kindsville into a beacon of kindness. Acts of kindness became an integral part of the town's culture, and smiles were exchanged freely among neighbors, friends, and strangers.

The story of Kindsville was a reminder to the world that acts of kindness and smiles extended beyond personal gratification. It celebrated the idea that the power of kindness lay in its ability to create a connected and caring community. It was a story that showcased the extraordinary ripple effect of kindness and the role of smiles in spreading warmth and goodwill to all.

Chapter Twenty three

The Neurological Impact of Smiles

In the bustling city of Neuroville, where scientific innovation and discovery were a way of life, there was a story about the profound impact of smiles on the human brain. This was a place where neuroscience and the art of smiling came together, revealing a remarkable insight into the neurological impact of smiles.

At the forefront of this story was Dr. Sophia Bennett, a brilliant neuroscientist with a lifelong fascination for smiles. Dr. Bennett had spent years exploring the complex relationship between facial expressions, emotions, and the human brain. Her journey began with a curiosity about the neurological impact of smiles and their potential to shape one's emotional well-being.

Dr. Bennett's research focused on several key discoveries that revealed the neurological impact of smiles:

1. **Endorphin Release:** Dr. Bennett found that the act of smiling triggered the release of endorphins, the brain's natural mood enhancers. These neurotransmitters induced feelings of happiness and reduced stress, providing an immediate emotional boost.

2. **Emotion Regulation:** Smiles had the power to regulate and modulate emotions. When individuals smiled, even if they didn't initially feel happy, their brain's emotional centers were influenced to adopt a more positive state.

3. **Stress Reduction:** The act of smiling reduced the release of stress hormones, such as cortisol, leading to a calmer and more relaxed state.

4. **Enhanced Social Bonds:** Smiles stimulated the brain's reward centers, encouraging social interaction and the formation of social bonds. This strengthened connections and fostered a sense of belonging.

5. **Positive Feedback Loop:** Dr. Bennett's research suggested that consistent smiling could create a positive feedback loop. The more a person smiled, the more their brain rewire itself to default to a positive emotional state.

The culmination of Dr. Bennett's work had far-reaching implications. It was evident that the neurological impact of smiles went beyond mere expressions of happiness. It was a powerful tool that could be harnessed to enhance emotional well-being, reduce stress, and foster positive relationships.

Neuroville became a hub for the study of the neurological impact of smiles. Dr. Bennett's research inspired a new generation of scientists to explore the brain's incredible potential for change through something as simple as a smile.

The story of Neuroville highlighted the extraordinary link between neuroscience and the art of smiling. It was a reminder to the world that smiles were not just gestures of happiness; they were tools that could actively shape one's emotional and neurological well-being. It was a story that celebrated the profound impact of smiles on the human brain and the incredible potential for positive change they held.

Chapter Twenty Four

The Link Between Smiles and Productivity

In the modern, bustling city of Prodigyville, where productivity and efficiency were highly prized, there was a remarkable story that delved into the intriguing link between smiles and productivity. It was a place where the workforce had recognized the profound impact of happiness and smiles on their ability to achieve exceptional results.

At the heart of Prodigyville was a visionary leader named Alex. Alex was the CEO of an innovative tech company, Pinnacle Solutions. Alex believed that the key to unlocking the full potential of the workforce lay in understanding and harnessing the connection between smiles and productivity.

Alex's journey to uncover the link between smiles and productivity began during a particularly challenging time for Pinnacle Solutions. The company was facing tough competition and dealing with high levels of stress and burnout among its employees. Productivity had plateaued, and innovation had stagnated.

In search of a solution, Alex initiated a comprehensive research project to explore the connection between smiles and productivity. Here's what they discovered:

1. **Mood Elevation:** Smiles had a direct impact on mood. When employees smiled, they experienced an elevation in their mood, which translated to higher levels of enthusiasm and motivation for work.

2. **Stress Reduction:** Smiles reduced stress levels. Employees who smiled experienced a drop in cortisol, the stress hormone, which allowed them to focus better on their tasks.

3. **Creativity and Problem-Solving:** Smiles enhanced creativity and problem-solving abilities. A positive mood facilitated thinking "outside the box" and innovative solutions to challenges.

4. **Team Cohesion:** Smiles improved team dynamics. When team members shared smiles, it created a sense of camaraderie and cooperation, making teamwork more effective.

5. **Increased Engagement:** Smiles fostered higher levels of engagement. Employees who were happier at work were more committed and willing to go the extra mile to achieve success.

Armed with these findings, Alex implemented several changes at Pinnacle Solutions:

1. Smiles as a Culture: The company embraced a culture of smiles and positivity. Employees were encouraged to start meetings with a smile and share success stories with one another.

2. Employee Well-Being: Pinnacle Solutions invested in employee well-being programs, such as mindfulness and stress management, to support emotional health and happiness.

3. Employee Recognition: The company implemented a peer recognition program where employees could nominate their colleagues for their achievements, celebrating them with a "Smile of Appreciation" award.

The transformation at Pinnacle Solutions was nothing short of remarkable. Productivity skyrocketed, and the work environment became a hub of innovation and creativity. Employees no longer viewed their work as a burden but as an opportunity for personal and professional growth.

The story of Prodigyville served as a reminder to the world that the link between smiles and productivity was not just a theory but a practical reality. It was a story that celebrated the power of happiness and the profound impact of smiles on achieving exceptional results, both for individuals and organizations.

Chapter Twenty Five
Smiles and Conflict Resolution

In the bustling city of Harmonyville, where people from diverse backgrounds and cultures coexisted, there was a remarkable story that explored the incredible role of smiles in conflict resolution. Harmonyville was known for its harmonious coexistence, and this story highlighted how smiles served as powerful tools for resolving disputes and maintaining peace.

At the heart of this story was Maria, a skilled mediator and peace advocate. Maria had always been fascinated by the potential for smiles to bridge gaps, build understanding, and resolve conflicts. She firmly believed that a genuine smile could be the first step towards resolving even the most challenging disputes.

Maria's journey to understanding the connection between smiles and conflict resolution began when she was assigned to mediate a long-standing conflict between two rival neighborhood associations. The dispute had festered for years, leading to tension, misunderstandings, and even occasional confrontations.

Maria approached the mediation session with a fresh perspective. She understood that effective conflict resolution was not just about addressing the issues at hand but also about mending strained relationships and fostering an atmosphere of trust and cooperation. Here's how Maria's approach led to a successful resolution:

1. Setting the Tone: Maria began the mediation session with a warm and welcoming smile. Her genuine demeanor immediately put the participants at ease and signaled her intention to create a positive and non-adversarial environment.

2. Active Listening: Maria listened attentively to both sides, ensuring that each party felt heard and validated. She made sure to acknowledge their concerns with empathy and a reassuring smile.

3. Smiles as Icebreakers: Whenever tensions ran high or the conversation became heated, Maria would interject with a light-hearted comment or a smile, diffusing the tension and encouraging a more constructive dialogue.

4. Finding Common Ground: Through her expert mediation, Maria helped the opposing parties identify common ground and shared goals. She encouraged them to focus on their shared interests rather than their differences.

5. Encouraging Empathy: Maria asked participants to put themselves in each other's shoes, fostering empathy and understanding. She often used her smile to convey a sense of unity and shared humanity.

As the mediation process unfolded, it became clear that smiles were not just expressions of friendliness but also essential tools for resolving conflicts. The participants gradually shifted from hostility to cooperation, and the dispute that had lasted for years began to unravel.

Through Maria's guidance and the power of smiles, the rival neighborhood associations not only reached a peaceful resolution but also developed a newfound sense of camaraderie. They realized that their shared community and a commitment to understanding one another were more important than their differences.

The story of Harmonyville was a testament to the profound impact of smiles on conflict resolution. It served as a reminder that even in the most challenging disputes, a genuine smile and a positive demeanor could be transformative tools for fostering understanding, building bridges, and achieving peace.

Chapter Twenty Six

Smiles and Goal Achievement

In the dynamic city of Achievementville, where ambition and determination were celebrated, there was an inspiring story about the role of smiles in achieving goals. This was a place where dreams were pursued relentlessly, and the residents understood that smiles played a pivotal role in realizing their aspirations.

At the center of this story was a young woman named Lily. Lily had always been an ambitious individual with a clear vision of her life goals. She was driven and determined, but she realized that her journey to success had been missing something essential: a positive attitude and genuine smiles.

Lily's realization came when she was pursuing her dream of becoming a renowned photographer. She had faced numerous challenges in her path—rejections, tight deadlines, and competition. Her unwavering determination had carried her through many obstacles, but it had also left her feeling stressed and drained.

One day, while reviewing her work, she noticed that her earlier photographs, those taken with joy and enthusiasm, stood out. The subjects in those photos seemed to come alive, radiating positivity, and evoking a sense of connection. The pictures taken during more stressful times, on the other hand, lacked the same charm and impact.

Lily embarked on a journey to understand the role of smiles in achieving her goals:

1. Mindset Shift: Lily realized that a positive mindset was crucial. She began each day with a smile and a positive affirmation, setting the tone for a successful and joyful day.

2. Embracing Failures: She learned to embrace failures with a smile. Rather than being discouraged, she saw them as opportunities for growth and improvement.

3. Building Relationships: Lily understood that genuine smiles fostered strong connections. She started building relationships with clients and colleagues based on trust and authenticity, which helped her career flourish.

4. Increased Resilience: Lily's positive outlook and frequent smiles made her more resilient in the face of challenges. She was able to bounce back from setbacks and continue working towards her goals with enthusiasm.

5. Celebrating Achievements: Lily celebrated her achievements with a sense of joy and gratitude. Each milestone reached was marked with a smile, which motivated her to set new, even more ambitious goals.

As Lily incorporated these changes into her life and her photography, the impact was profound. Her work took on a new vibrancy, and her career began to flourish. Her clients not only admired her talent but also appreciated her positivity and approachability.

The story of Achievementville was a reminder that the journey to success was not just about determination and hard work; it was also about embracing a positive attitude and genuine smiles. It celebrated the idea that smiles were not just expressions of happiness but also tools for fostering resilience, building relationships, and achieving one's most ambitious goals.